CREATE YOUR OWN

WEBSITE OR BLOG

Matt Anniss

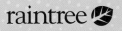

raintree

a Capstone company — publishers for children

Raintree is an imprint of Capstone Global Library Limited, a company incorporated in England and Wales having its registered office at 264 Banbury Road, Oxford, OX2 7DY – Registered company number: 6695582

www.raintree.co.uk
myorders@raintree.co.uk

Edited by James Benefield and Helen Cox Cannons
Designed by Steve Mead
Original illustrations © Capstone Global Library Ltd 2016
Picture research by Morgan Walters
Production by Victoria Fitzgerald
Originated by Capstone Global Library
Printed and bound in China

ISBN 978 1 474 71375 7 (hardback)
20 19 18 17 16
10 9 8 7 6 5 4 3 2 1

ISBN 978 1 474 71384 9 (paperback)
21 20 19 18 17
10 9 8 7 6 5 4 3 2 1

British Library Cataloguing in Publication Data
A full catalogue record for this book is available from the British Library.

Acknowledgements
The author and publisher are grateful to the following for permission to reproduce copyright material: Corbis: C. Devan, 18, David Deas/DK Stock, 14, David Woods, 34, Hiya Images, 4; Getty Images: Jeff Vespa, 28; iStockphoto: PeopleImages, cover; Newscom: Michael Quan/ZUMAPRESS, 5; Shutterstock: A-R-T, 41, Alexey V Smirnov, 33, Angela Hawkey, 36, Annette Shaff, 9, Asmati Chibalashvili, 31, bikeriderlondon, 10, Brothers Good, design element 27, Dan Kosmayer, 19, Denis Kuvaev, 26, Denis Makarenko, 39, dotshock, 32, Ekaterina Brusnika, bottom middle 6, Golden Pixels LLC, 8, gst, design element 27, Jag_cz, 20-21, Javier Brosch, top left 6, jirasaki, 29, Mary Rice, (white dog) middle right 6, PathDoc, 12, Peshkova, 42, Pressmaster, 43, rebeccaashworth, (dog run) bottom left 6, Rob Marmion, 16, ShaunWilkinson, 7, Stephen Coburn, 23, Tyler Olson, 15, Vladvm, design element 27, wavebreakmedia, 38, 40; Syed Balkhi, 37; Wikimedia: Joi, 24

We would like to thank Killian Czuba for her invaluable help in the preparation of this book.

Every effort has been made to contact copyright holders of material reproduced in this book. Any omissions will be rectified in subsequent printings if notice is given to the publisher.

All the internet addresses (URLs) given in this book were valid at the time of going to press. However, due to the dynamic nature of the internet, some addresses may have changed, or sites may have changed or ceased to exist since publication. While the author and publisher regret any inconvenience this may cause readers, no responsibility for any such changes can be accepted by either the author or the publisher.

Contents

Your home on the
INTERNET!

The internet, and specifically the World Wide Web, gives people amazing opportunities to be creative. For example, anyone with a few ideas can sit down and create a website or a blog. A website is a collection of specially formatted documents, known as web pages. A blog is just one main, continuous page – although there can be links to other pages. A blog is also more interactive than a website. It allows readers to comment on, or somehow interact with, the content.

Starting a website or blog is a great thing to do with friends. It means you can all easily share the funny, cool and interesting things you've found online.

Wonderful Web

So what exactly is the World Wide Web, or the Web for short? It's basically an ever-growing collection of web pages, blogs and websites. The Web can be accessed by any device connected to the internet, using an application called a web browser. The Web forms just one part of the internet. Simply, the internet is a network that connects over 3 billion computers and mobile devices around the world.

The Web is the world's biggest collaborative project. To date, millions of people have contributed to it by starting their own blogs and websites. Have you ever thought about taking part? Maybe you'd like to share your writing, showcase great photos you've taken, or simply want to talk about your favourite subject. Whatever your inspiration, creating a blog or website is a good way to share it with others.

THE KNOWLEDGE

We take the Web for granted, but it's only been part of our lives since 1990. That year, British computer scientist Tim Berners-Lee invented a coding language for creating and displaying content over the internet. This was Hypertext Markup Language (HTML), and it allowed him to produce the world's first website.

CHAPTER 1

What makes a good WEBSITE or BLOG?

Before you can dive into making a website or blog, you need to decide which type of site suits you.

Websites

Today, there are few people who haven't visited a website at some point. Websites are organized into sections, which in turn can contain any number of web pages. These sections are usually accessed through a home page (this is the page that you see first when you visit a website), and menus at the top and bottom of each individual web page. Websites are great as they can be any size you want. They can also contain interactive elements, such as videos, games and animations, as well as words and pictures. Websites are more complicated to create than blogs, but offer more opportunities to be creative.

All About Dogs!

CANINE NEWS   DOG SHOWS   BREEDS   YOUR DOGS   CONTACT US

WELCOME TO ALL ABOUT DOGS!
We love dogs, and we know you do, too. That's why you've visited our site. Click on the links above to check out the different sections of the site. We've got a packed news section featuring interesting stories from around the doggie world, a section dedicated to dog shows – in case you want to enter your prize-winning pooch – and information on different types of breeds. The "Your Dogs" section includes pictures you've sent in of your pets. If you'd like to submit an image, click on 'contact us'.

Dog Shows
All the news and results from competitions around the world, plus our

Breeds
If you don't know a Spaniel from a Schnauzer, or a Collie from a Chihuahua, this

DOG OF THE WEEK!

Dog of the Week
This week's dog of the week is Rex, whose owner Claire sent in this picture of the two

LATEST NEWS

Crufts set to be BIGGEST dog show yet!
This year's Crufts will be the biggest dog show the world has ever seen, according to the organizers.
Click here to read more >>

Success Story

Juliette Brindak was just 10 years old when she created the Miss O and Friends cartoon characters. Over the next few years, she developed the idea for a website based on her characters. By 2008, three years after the site launched, Juliette's website business was valued at a massive £9.5 million ($14.7 million)!

Blogs

Blogs are a simple type of website. When you visit a blog, you'll see a single page featuring a short series of posts. These are articles containing writing, pictures, videos, sounds and interactive elements. The most recent posts are displayed at the top. Blogs are made by people called bloggers, who regularly update their sites. When blogs started in the mid-1990s, they took the form of online diaries. Today, a blog is usually the work of one or two people, who add new posts whenever inspiration strikes. Blogs are a good choice if you want to write regularly, as they're quick to create and easy to update.

Bees and Butterflies

ABOUT

POSTS

Wednesday, 18 April

Colourful butterfly spotted
I saw this amazing butterfly today. It looked a little bit like this:

Tuesday, 17 April

Pond problems
I went to the local pond today to find some wildlife. But instead this is what I saw:
- Lots of litter in the pond
- A broken gate at the entrance

POSTS

REVIEWS
JANUARY
FEBRUARY
MARCH
APRIL
MAY
JUNE
JULY

LINKS

Should I make a blog?

There are a number of things to consider when deciding whether you should create a blog. First and foremost, how often will you want to add new content? It's an important question. People expect blogs to deliver updates daily or weekly. Websites can be updated just as regularly, but they don't need to be. Some websites stay the same, or similar, for months on end.

Do your research

Before you decide, check out some blogs for yourself. You can find lists of interesting blogs on websites called blog directories. As you move between blogs, make a note of any features that you keep seeing, and anything that makes the best blogs stand out. Perhaps you can use some of the features you see on your blog.

The best blog posts get people talking, sparking conversation and attracting more visitors to the blog.

Some blogs cover lots of different subjects, but the most popular ones are usually focused on a very specific topic. You'll even find blogs entirely made up of funny pictures of animals!

The secrets of blogging success

So what have you noticed? Here are a few things that might come up:

> Many of the most popular blogs are updated regularly, with posts being added at least once a day – sometimes more often.

> Lots of blog posts have comments appearing underneath them that are from their readers. This feature can be a sign of a popular blog. If there are lots of comments, it means readers want to talk about what's being written.

> Each blogger has his or her own particular writing style. Some people are chatty and funny, while others are serious and considered.

Many popular websites are a little like newspapers or magazines, with different types of articles organized into sections.

STAY SAFE

The Web contains some great information, but anyone can publish anything online. This means you never quite know what you'll find. It is for this reason that you should ask an adult for permission to go online. Ask for an adult's help if you are not sure where to find what you need. When searching the internet, always use a safe search engine, such as Safe Search Kids.

Should I make a website?

When you get a moment, check out a few websites, taking note of what you find. Look at things you like and dislike, and features that crop up time and time again. The first thing you may notice is that, unlike blogs, there is no standard layout or look to websites. Even so, the finest websites often have a fairly simple design to help users find their way around easily.

SECRETS OF WEBSITE SUCCESS

What else did you notice? Here are some common traits of successful websites:

1 Websites often cover subjects in much greater detail than blogs, with sections dedicated to different topics or types of writing.

2 Websites can be the work of a team of writers and designers, or just one or two people.

3 Great websites have a target readership. That means they're aimed at certain types of people, for example teenagers, parents, music fans or film fans.

4 Websites are often more interactive than blogs. Websites might have games to play, videos to watch and sounds to listen to.

5 Popular websites feature content that makes people want to come back and visit on a regular basis.

CHAPTER 2

Planning your WEBSITE or BLOG

Although starting a website or blog is a quick process, it can take some time to get it right. That's why it pays to spend time researching and planning before you begin.

Before you decide between creating a blog or a website, you need to think carefully about your choices. What do you want to achieve? Which format suits all of your aims?

Fools rush in

Statistics show that most bloggers don't spend enough time planning their blogs ahead of starting them. According to a study of 133 million blogs, only 7.4 million had been updated in the past four months. The study found that around 95 per cent of bloggers quit within a few months of starting their blogs. Without planning and clear direction, your blog or website could go the same way.

QUIZ
Blog or website?

If you're still struggling to make up your mind, this multiple-choice quiz should help.

Which of the following do you most agree with?

A I'd like to create something that reflects my personality.

B I'm really interested in a subject and would like to cover it in depth.

What's the big idea?

Picking a subject or angle for your blog or website is of huge importance. It needs to be something that you feel passionate about. You'll need passion as you should have the drive to keep updating the blog or website even months after starting it. Some people choose to focus on a hobby or favourite subject, while others write about many different topics in an unusual way. Whichever approach you decide to take, it's important to have a clear vision from the start.

Some people don't write blog posts; they create short videos instead! This approach is known as vlogging (short for video blogging).

What's your USP?

Many of the best blogs and websites have a unique selling point, or USP for short. This is something that helps them stand out from the crowd. This could be covering subjects that nobody else does, or approaching a popular topic from a different angle.

For example, there are loads of blogs and websites about music. However, not many of these focus on little-known styles of music. There are loads of sites about how pop stars look, but not as many about the music-making process, such as songwriting. Offering something that nobody else does is the ultimate aim – how you achieve this is up to you.

Success Story

When he was 15, Alex Fraiser started a blog with a USP. His blog, **www.blogussion.com**, focused on the art of successful blogging and offered tips to other would-be bloggers. By early 2010, Blogussion had over 20,000 subscribers (they're people who get automatic updates on new posts). This made the site the world's most popular blog by a person of his age at the time.

If you find a USP you will create a lot of interest in your blog. Try to think of a popular subject and present it in a fresh way.

Coming up with content ideas is just a matter of thinking creatively. If your blog or website is about food, you could post recipes, restaurant reviews or interviews with chefs.

Final preparations

On the internet, "content is king". This means great content is the secret behind attracting people to your blog or website and turning them into regular visitors. To create great content, you should first of all provide something that is factually correct. Check all your facts in at least two places. Also, you should provide new information or a new spin on older information.

Something else to consider is how frequently you're going to update your blog or website. Regardless of how great your content is, people are more likely to return if your blog or website is updated regularly. Try doing this several times a week. New updates don't always need to contain lots of new information.

Since making a blog or website can be very time-consuming, ask your friends and classmates to get involved. Many of the most successful blogs and websites are created by a group of people with shared interests, rather than just one person.

PLAN OF ACTION ✔

Try making a plan for what you're going to feature on your blog or website over the first few weeks:

✔ Try to come up with five to ten great ideas for content that you could include when you create the blog or website. If you're struggling, try your hand at different types of writing. You could write a "comment piece" expressing an opinion about a hot topic, preview a forthcoming event, film, TV show or music release, or even interview somebody you find interesting.

✔ Take these ideas and expand on what could be covered in each. For example, if you're covering new music, you could talk about different genres or perhaps new releases.

✔ It might help to make an "update diary", noting down when you plan to add new content over the coming weeks and months. You can always change this plan slightly, or add extra updates if inspiration strikes!

CHAPTER 3

Creating a BLOG

While building a website is easier than it once was, thanks to templates and online tools, it's still much simpler to create a blog. That's because most blogging services are designed to let you create a blog in a matter of minutes.

Microblogging is a particularly quick way of blogging. This style of blogging is based around services such as Twitter, Tumblr and Pinterest. These services allow users to post short messages, or share cool things they've found on the internet. This could be anything from great articles, or short, looped animations known as animated GIFs. When sharing web content, users are encouraged to explain where they found it, so that the creators can get credit. This credit could be a link to the site where you found your content.

Pinterest and Tumblr are a little like online noticeboards. They allow users to store and share cool things they've found online.

First steps

Microblogging gets you used to the idea of making regular posts. You can write a few words on Twitter, post a picture to Tumblr or share a link on Pinterest in a matter of seconds. All you need to do is sign up for an account and follow the instructions. Within a few minutes you'll have made your first microblog post!

STAY SAFE

You must be at least 13 years old to sign up for an account with most microblogging services. If you are 13 or over and have started microblogging, never give out any personal information, such as your home address.

Pro Tip

Twitter is the most popular microblogging service out there, with over 236 million active users every month. Each microblog post, known as a "tweet", has a maximum length of 140 characters (letters, numbers, full stops, spaces, etc.). That's only a little longer than the first sentence of this tip box!

Many "microbloggers" use services such as Twitter to post updates while they're on the move, wherever they are in the world. This is made possible thanks to microblogging "apps" for smartphone and tablet.

Getting started

The first step in creating your blog is to sign up with a blog hosting service. These are websites that will give your blog a permanent home on the internet, free of charge. They also allow you to post new articles and manage the look of your blog, all through your web browser. Popular blog hosting services include Blogger, Wordpress, Typepad, LiveJournal and Blog.com.

Signing up for an account

Once you've chosen a hosting service, you'll need to find the sign-up option on the home page. Click on that, and you'll be asked to enter your name, an email address and sometimes a few other details. Whenever you need to give contact information out on the internet, ask an adult for permission first.

If microblogging has made you hungry for more, you're ready to start your very first blog!

As part of the sign-up process to a blog, you'll have to pick a name for your site. This name will form part of the address that people type into their web browser to visit your blog. Ideally, it should be memorable or catchy, so people remember the name. If it's something to do with the subject you're covering, even better. For example, there is a popular music review blog called Drowned In Sound. The name will be attached to the blog forever, so think hard!

You've got the look!

Once you've signed up for a blogging account, you can choose a look for your blog. Blogging services make this process simple, by offering you a choice of hundreds or even thousands of templates known as themes. Web designers create these themes with different types of blogs in mind. It's worth taking time to pick one that you think will suit your blog. Blog hosting services often allow you to switch between themes at any time, so you could always try a few out before deciding.

PICK A THEME

When you browse through potential themes on hosting sites, you'll notice that there are a huge number of styles to choose from. Usually, the main differences between the themes are:

> the layout of the blog
> the fonts used – this is the style and shape of the letters, and therefore affects how the text looks on the page
> the colours used for backgrounds and fonts
> the links or other things that appear around the edges of the page. These are sometimes called widgets. They contain things such as lists of previous posts (called archives) and links to other cool blogs or websites.

Some aspects, such as the fonts and colour scheme, can still be changed even after you've picked the theme.

Themes and subjects

There are an almost unlimited number of ways that you can customize your theme. However, most bloggers choose fonts, backgrounds and colours that suit the subject they're blogging about. So, a blog about heavy metal bands might have a black background, white text and red headlines, in keeping with the dark and loud feel of the music. Likewise, if your blog is about your favourite sports team, you could use colours that match their kit or uniforms.

Just like the way you can personalize your bedroom by putting up posters and pictures, you can tailor the look of your blog to reflect your personality and interests.

Writing your first blog post

Now that you've decided on a look for your blog, it's time to write your first post and become a blogger! Helpfully, blog hosting services make it really easy to do this. Once you've signed into the service, find the "new post" button and click on it. That should open up a new page containing an empty text box and a load of control buttons.

THE KNOWLEDGE

In 1999, three software designers in San Francisco, USA, created a Web-based system that made it easier for people to publish their own writing and pictures online. Inspired by a new trend for "weblogs", they called it Blogger.com. Within three years, hundreds of thousands of people were using it to create their own blogs. By 2003, it was so popular that Google decided to buy the website.

Pro Tip

Many bloggers use their first post to welcome readers to their blog, and explain what it's all about. This is a smart move, as it gives their readers a taste of what's to come. Don't forget to be enthusiastic. You want people to come back and check what you're posting on a regular basis!

Internet businessman Evan Williams has done more than almost anyone else to make blogging popular. He was one of the co-founders of the Blogger.com service. He later went on to help invent the popular microblogging network Twitter.

BLOGGING BASICS

Title box
This is where you add the attention-grabbing headline that will draw people to your post.

Text formatting tools
Click on these buttons to change the look of your text so that it stands out. You can. for example. make text bold.

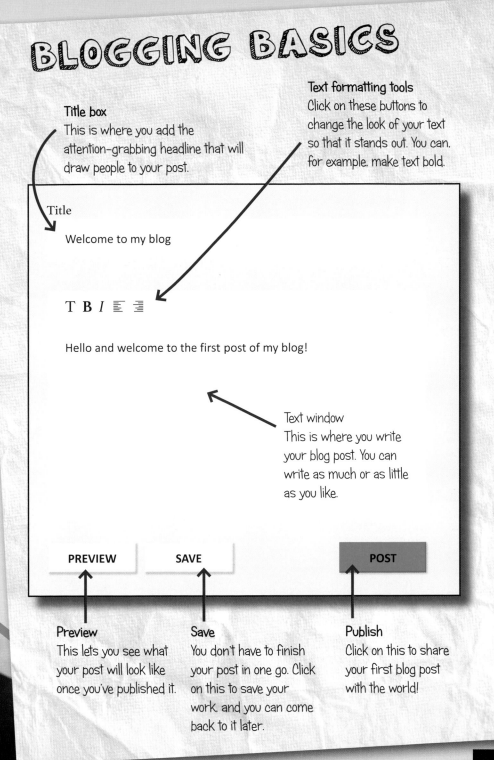

Title

Welcome to my blog

T **B** *I* ☰ ☰

Hello and welcome to the first post of my blog!

Text window
This is where you write your blog post. You can write as much or as little as you like.

PREVIEW   SAVE   POST

Preview
This lets you see what your post will look like once you've published it.

Save
You don't have to finish your post in one go. Click on this to save your work. and you can come back to it later.

Publish
Click on this to share your first blog post with the world!

Some bloggers use their blogs to showcase their photography or artistic skills, as well as their way with words.

Making multimedia posts

Blog posts don't have to be limited to writing. Hosting services for blogs provide tools for adding different types of content to your posts, to make your blog more interesting and attract more visitors. Try using some of the following popular multimedia elements:

It is illegal to upload other people's music, films and TV shows to the internet. They are protected by copyright, which means you are not allowed to share them without the owner's permission. However, you can include links to streaming video or music sites, such as YouTube, SoundCloud and Mixcloud. These services pay a fee to copyright holders to make these clips available over the internet.

Pictures

These brighten up the page or illustrate what you've written. You could take your own snaps. If you want to use photos you've found online you must check copyright details – you may have to pay a fee to the photographer or artist whose work you are using. And you will have to mention their name (called crediting).

Videos

Again, make your own or include ones you've found on video sharing sites. As before, credit the website it came from and the original creator if it's someone else's work.

Music

If you make your own music, or your friends write songs, you could include some in your blog posts. See the Pro Tip box (above) for some rules on sharing music online.

Links

Include links to take your readers to another blog or website. They can be used to provide more information on a subject, or encourage people to visit a website you like.

Polls

These allow your readers to vote on a question related to the topic or the blog itself. They are a great way of encouraging readers to engage with your blog posts.

CHAPTER 4

Websites for BEGINNERS

As great as blogs are, they don't offer anywhere near as much room for creativity as websites. Blogs are usually based around one central page, with bloggers adding different multimedia elements as they see fit within that page. There are often places for readers to comment over content.

Websites, on the other hand, are a blank canvas. You have total control of every aspect – not just the look and feel, but also how everything is structured and arranged. The only limit is your imagination. You can have a blog as part of a website, too.

Success Story

Tavi Gevinson started her own fashion blog, Style Rookie, when she was 11 years old. At the age of 14, she turned this into a fully fledged website and online magazine, called *Rookie*. Within five days of launching, the *Rookie* website had attracted well over a million visitors!

Different arrangement

On a website, content is included on a number of different pages, which can then be arranged into sections. These sections can be based on themes, subjects or the style of content. For example, if you made a website for your football team, it could include the following sections:

- Latest news
- Match reports
- Results and fixtures
- Photo gallery
- Videos of the team in action

Putting together all these different sections makes building a website more time-consuming than writing a blog, but it can be far more satisfying.

Creating a website is a little like solving a jigsaw puzzle. Many elements slot together to make the finished article.

Planning your website

When it comes to building your first website, the planning stage is of huge importance. That's because you need to think about what pages you're going to include, the content featured on them and how you might arrange them. Once you've done this, you can go about creating the website, possibly in a few hours.

Preparing your website

With a blog, you can add content as you go along. You can start with a single post and then write more over the following days and weeks. If you're building a website, it needs to include plenty of good content from the moment it goes online. You'll need to prepare this before you build the website. If you do, it will speed up the process of creating pages.

Preparing content beforehand isn't as complicated as you think. Firstly, you can write it in a word processing application. This way, the content won't disappear if your internet connection fails. It also means you can spellcheck what you write! You can then save the document to your computer and add it to the web pages as you make them.

THE KNOWLEDGE

If you enjoy creating your first website, perhaps you could consider a future career in web design? Professional web designers specialize in building and running websites. They have a flair for eye-catching design, an understanding of what makes a good website, and an impressive understanding of the software used to build them. This software is updated often, so the best web designers are constantly learning new things.

Arranging your website

Before you start building a website, you need to work out the sections and pages you're going to include. At this time, it's also useful to think about how they join together. People need to be able to find their way around your site easily, without getting lost. Perhaps the best way to work this out is to get a piece of paper and draw out a rough sketch of your sections and pages. Start with the home page at the top, with the sections and pages as shown.

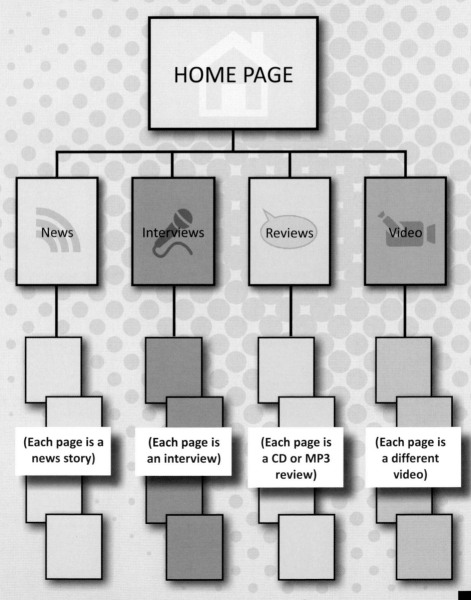

HOME PAGE

News

Interviews

Reviews

Video

(Each page is a news story)

(Each page is an interview)

(Each page is a CD or MP3 review)

(Each page is a different video)

Creating a website from scratch

There are two main ways of building a website. The first is to create it from scratch offline using web design software. In this method, web designers use a combination of arranging things on a page and a computer coding language called HTML (or its big brother, the more recent HTML5). Once the site is ready, it's then uploaded to the internet for people to view. If you choose this method, you'll need to sign up with a web hosting service, many of which offer web space for free.

When you upload a website to a hosting service, your files are held on special storage computers called web servers.

Creating a website quickly

If learning web design seems a little too complicated, you could try using an online website building service. With this method, you create a site through your web browser, simply by picking a template, dragging and dropping elements, and inserting your own text and pictures. These services are quick, easy and don't require any previous knowledge of coding. Popular, free or inexpensive web building services include Squarespace, Wix, Moonfruit, Yola and Weebly.

THE KNOWLEDGE

HTML is a basic computer coding language used to create web pages and sites. Coders use a series of standardized instructions called HTML tags, which are written into a document known as the source code (see photo, below). The source code tells the web browser how to display the contents of the page when you visit it. You can find out more about HTML and learn how tags work at the Code Academy website.

All products, from cars to toys, are rigorously tested before being sold to the public. Websites go through a testing process, too, to make sure that they work and display everything properly.

Testing your website

Once you've built your website, it's a good idea to test it out before you publish it on the internet. A good way to do this is to get a friend, classmate, parent or teacher to try the site. Ask them to check whether all the links work, so that when they click on a link, the right page appears. Those that don't work are known as broken links, and you would want to fix these before launching your site.

Editing your website

Once a website has been launched, you can change – or edit – it as much as you want. You can add and remove pages, and tweak those already uploaded. How you edit your website depends on the way you created it:

- If you made the website from scratch using web design software, you will have to edit the pages offline, on your computer. Once you're happy with the new pages, simply upload your website to the server again. This will replace your old website with the shiny new version.

- If you used an online website building tool, you can quickly make changes using the service's content management system (CMS for short). Blog hosting services use CMSs to allow bloggers to publish and edit their posts. The CMSs of most websites are very similar, and feature tools for formatting, adding and organizing web pages. It is also possible to create your own CMS from scratch, though this is very complicated.

THE KNOWLEDGE

All computer programs, including those used to build and edit websites, are based on algorithms. These are procedures or formulas used to solve problems. They describe the process the computer has to go through in order to complete a task. All computers and electronic devices use algorithms. CMSs also use algorithms to run the database that stores your website and web pages.

Basic flowchart

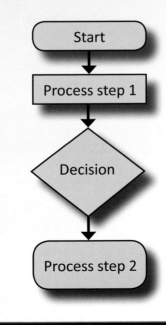

CHAPTER 5

Developing your WEBSITE or BLOG

Don't worry if your website or blog isn't perfect. You can keep altering it and adding content to it until you're happy. Once you are happy with your site, you can start looking at how you might develop it further.

Your website or blog should reflect your personality. Whether you're passionate, funny, easy-going or serious about issues, let the world know!

Keep updating

The fastest way to web success is to ensure that your blog or website is updated regularly – at least a few times a week. Adding new content gives readers a reason to return to your site. The more people share your content with each other via social media, the higher your website ranking is likely to be on search engines like Bing or Google.

Finding your voice

Apart from having a USP for their website, the most successful bloggers and web writers also have a unique voice. This is a way of writing that reflects their personality and engages with readers. If your blog or website is going to be a success, you'll need to develop an appealing style and tone of writing that keeps people coming back for more. You can find your voice by trying out different styles of writing, until you find one that you're comfortable with.

Success Story

Syed Balkhi was 12 years old when he built his first website. During his teenage years, he founded a successful web design company, Uzzz Productions, as well as launching WPBeginner, a website that helps bloggers get started on Wordpress.

Building an audience

Over 3 billion people worldwide now use the internet. How are you going to get some of those people to check out your website, and hopefully come back for more?

Think about who would enjoy reading your blog or website. Are they kids, teenagers or adults, or a mixture of all three? Is it just for people with a passion for a particular hobby, or anyone who wants to be entertained? Once you've worked out your potential readership, you can then try to attract them to your blog or website.

There are millions of potential website visitors out there. You just need to find ways of attracting visitors to your site – and then turn them into regular readers.

Want to attract more people to your site? Try posting regular articles that tie in with the release of popular films or things happening in the news.

Gather ideas on how to find and build an audience, noting down anything you come up with on a piece of paper. Here are a few ideas to get you started:

- Look at a number of websites covering your subject. See what they do well and see if you can do it better.
- Write articles that spark debate, and ask readers to leave their comments underneath.
- Invite your regular readers to publish on your blog or website. Include people who comment a lot, to make them feel like they're an important part of your site.
- Ask readers to fill in a short survey, saying what they like and dislike about the site.

The fastest way to gain readers is to publicize your blog or website, either online or in the real world. Sticking up posters at school is a good place to start.

Publicizing your blog or website

Businesses spend huge amounts of money on advertising and other schemes to try to get people to visit their websites. According to one report, companies spent around $590 billion (£389 billion) in 2015 on advertising campaigns worldwide!

This is what's known as marketing, and most bloggers and website creators do it. Most, though, don't spend any money. Instead, they rely on free tricks of the trade, from emailing friends and family to word of mouth. In other words, never underestimate the power of your friends and family passing information along to their friends!

Social media marketing

One of the most popular tools for online marketing is social media, and particularly networks such as Facebook and Twitter. You could set up profile pages for your site on Facebook and Twitter, then invite friends to "like" them. Once they do, they'll get updates when you post a link to one of your articles or web pages.

STAY SAFE

You have to be at least 13 years of age to sign up with social networks such as Facebook. Once you're old enough, and have an adult's permission, you can explore and use all of the privacy settings. That way, people you don't know can't see what you post.

Like

If someone likes an article of yours on social media, they may share it on their profile page. The more an article is shared, the more likely a higher number of people will read it.

Just the beginning!

You should now have the information you need to start your own blog or build a website. If not, take your time – there's no rush. Once you've got into it, you may well find it addictive. Before you know it, you may be spending all of your spare time updating your site!

Lifelong learning

And why wouldn't you? Blogging and website building are really fun hobbies. They allow you the creative freedom to indulge your interests while also entertaining and informing others. If you're bored with the way your site looks, or want to change the way you write about a subject, just do it – it's your project, after all.

The more you blog or update your website, the more you'll learn about the technical aspects – things like HTML, CMS and online marketing. You'll also learn more about what type of content attracts the most readers, and whether it makes a difference adding pictures or video clips. Within months, you'll be a real internet whizz!

Knowledge is power

If you enjoy working with blogs and websites, you might be able to turn it into a career, just like those young people featured in the Success Stories in this book have done. As well as careers in web design, there are jobs for web writers, content creators and marketers, who publicize websites and online services.

That's for the future. Over the next few months and years, you may be able to turn your blog or website into a profitable, moneymaking business. However you decide to use your new skills, and whatever direction you take your blog or website in, your journey has just begun!

Skills you learn as a blogger or web writer are much in demand today, especially in the media. When you're older, they could help land you a job working on a website, magazine or newspaper.

Glossary

algorithm set of instructions that tell a computer or other electronic device the process it must go through to complete a specific task

angle particular way of presenting a subject

coder someone who creates code, for example a web designer who uses HTML to create and format websites

coding language sometimes called a markup language, this is a set of instructions, usually in the form of key words and phrases, used to tell software applications how to format, or display, content. The web coding language, HTML, tells a web browser how to display web pages.

debate exchange of views between people who hold differing opinions

hosting service company that offers both free storage space and the tools to create some blogs and websites

HTML short for Hypertext Markup Language, a coding language used to create web pages

HTML5 most recent version of HTML, which gives web designers more options to include things like video, sounds and animation

interactive in computing, something is said to be interactive if it responds to commands from a user. Interactive elements on blogs or websites are those that respond when you click on something, or, occasionally, move the mouse cursor over a certain part of the page.

link reference to another document, such as a blog post or web page, stored elsewhere on the World Wide Web. Clicking on one takes you to the linked document.

marketing process of raising awareness of a product or service in order to attract more customers or visitors

microblog type of blog where users can only post short messages, photographs, videos or other web content

multimedia term to describe websites that combine text with any combination of video, sounds, pictures, animations, games or interactive elements

search engine website that allows you to search the internet for websites, blogs and information on any subject you can think of

software computer program designed for a specific purpose, for example designing web pages

tag command inserted by coders into a document that specifies how the document, or a particular part of it, should be formatted. In web design, coders use HTML tags to tell browsers how to display web pages.

template document, for example a web page, with a predetermined structure and appearance, which can then be modified

theme set of templates used to determine the appearance of a blog

web browser software used to locate, retrieve and display information on the World Wide Web, specifically websites and web pages

web server storage computer built specifically to store web pages and websites. All websites are stored on a server. When you visit a blog or website, your browser retrieves the information it needs to display the pages directly from the site's web server.

word processing application software program that allows you to write, edit and save text documents, for example Microsoft Word or Apple's Pages

Find out more

Books

Start a Blog (Find Your Talent), Matt Anniss (Franklin Watts, 2014)
Web Design with HTML5 (Makers as Innovators), Colleen Van Lent (Cherry Lake
   Publishing, 2014)
What is a Website and How Do I Use It? (Practical Technology), Matt Anniss
   (Rosen Education, 2014)

Websites

Code Academy
www.codeacademy.com
If you're interested in learning about coding – an important part of computer
programming – this should be your first port of call. It features easy-to-follow
tutorials on lots of different coding languages, including HTML.

The History of the World Wide Web
www.webfoundation.org/about/vision/history-of-the-web
Find out more about how Tim Berners-Lee created the World Wide Web in this
quick history lesson from the World Wide Web Foundation.

Liquid Design – Free Web Templates
www.freeliquidtemplates.com
If you fancy building your own website from scratch, these templates could
prove very helpful. Combine these with a basic knowledge of HTML and you'll
have a great site in no time at all!

Safe Search Kids
www.safesearchkids.com
If you want to be sure of finding websites that don't contain any unsafe
material, this search engine is a great place to start.

Stage of Life Teen Blog Directory
www.stageoflife.com/StageHighSchool/OtherResources/
TeenBlogDirectory.aspx
This is a great directory of blogs created by other children and teenagers. If
you're stuck for inspiration, this should give you a few ideas!

Top Tips For Child Bloggers
www.jakes-bones.com/2012/08/my-top-ten-tips-for-other-
child-bloggers.html
Scottish blogger Jake was just a kid when he started his site. Here he offers some great tips for other young people who want to get into blogging.

Further research

There's no better resource for would-be bloggers and website creators than the World Wide Web itself. We've listed a few useful websites here, but there are many others packed with advice for aspiring web designers. Whether you're struggling with the basics of HTML, online marketing or any other aspect of the creative process, you'll find sites packed with step-by-step guides, tips and handy tricks. Because technology is constantly changing, you're also more likely to find up-to-date advice online, rather than in books.

Many community colleges and local education organizations offer workshops and courses in web design, many of which are aimed at children and young people. There are also plenty of companies that offer weekend and summer computer camps, where you can learn programming skills. Check your local listings for more information, or ask your teachers if they know of anything suitable.

If you think you might want to pursue a career in web design, you can find out more about the skills and qualifications you'll need online, too. The National Careers Service in the UK has some excellent advice on its website: https://nationalcareersservice.direct. gov.uk/advice/planning/jobprofiles/Pages/webdesigner.aspx

Once you've mastered running your own blog or website, volunteer to make one for a local community organization, club, or sports team. Alternatively, you could make a private website or blog (meaning only invited guests will have access) for your family, or extended friendship group. Once you've got the blogging or web design bug, there's no shortage of projects you could take on!

Index